HOW TO ATTRACT A MAN:

Secret Tips On How To Attract a Man You Love.

By Michelle W. Bartolome

Table Of Contents

Chapter 1

How to Attract Men

There are a few really true secrets about how to attract guys that no one ever discusses. Do you aspire to be the girl who can make any man swoon?

How do you approach men?

You may learn how to draw guys to you and quickly arouse their desire by using an evolutionary secret. And here is where the true secret is. It takes more than just a few hints or flirtatious gestures to pique a man's attention.

You'll see things in a whole different light if you comprehend the very genuine concept of attraction. Despite how difficult it may appear, it is rather easy to summarize the science of sex attraction in a few sentences.

What about a guy that appeals to you?

We've found through thousands of studies and research projects over the years that ladies are more drawn to men who seem healthy and stress-free, have a healthy amount of testosterone that makes him look more muscular and chiseled, and have a protective streak that makes him a wonderful partner and a parent.

On the other hand, because of their beauty or personalities, guys are more drawn to ladies.

But that isn't the case.

We must go further into the idea of attraction from the perspective of men if we are to properly comprehend how to attract guys and how a man thinks.

Getting men's attention in a manner they can't resist

For several reasons, a man could adore a lady. But her outward demeanor and physical attributes count more than anything else when it comes to physical or sexual attraction at first sight. I'm just being honest here. And everyone of us needs a place to build from.

So, all you have to do to capture a man's attention and make him want you is get his attention in the proper manner. You'll be sure to attract his attention right away if you read through these 22 techniques to grab a guy's attention in any situation.

But the important thing to keep in mind is this: and this is something you should remember. Attraction and love are two very different things. Even if a man finds you to be very seductive and appealing, he could not end up falling in love with you. There are factors that are significantly more crucial to a woman's attraction than just seeming "hot."

Of course, in order for love to begin, you must first develop a sexual attraction to him.He must, however, have an emotional connection to you in order for him to fall in love with you. If you're interested in learning more about how that works, read this article about how guys fall in love and the seven steps they go through before they do.

Attraction and a man's perception of a woman's physique

You need to comprehend what a man's mind tells him when he sees you and evaluates you sexually, since it is well known that physical appeal plays a significant role in enticing a guy.

A male instinctively takes in more of a girl's physical attributes than simply her breasts and butt. When a lady has the appropriate curves in the proper places, a man knows she's healthy, fertile, and of legal age because her body can afford to spend its energy on producing those curves, which are the main factor in sex attractiveness.

A woman may be considered attractive by a man. But he's subconsciously evaluating you as the potential future mother of his children. No matter whether you're seeking a fling or a companion, a guy will unconsciously look for these qualities in a woman if he plans to approach her.

An individual's sexual inclination and testosterone

In his testicles, every man generates the sexual hormone testosterone. And the ovaries of women create a modest quantity of testosterone. The more testosterone a guy generates, the more masculine and sexually active he seems to be. His voice is deeper, his jaws are wider and more defined, and his facial features appear more masculine.

Furthermore, several studies have shown that the more macho a woman is, the more males are drawn to her feminine features.If you're curious about what men find to be feminine and what they don't, here are 20 things that make a woman seem more feminine in their eyes.

On the other hand, a small percentage of men with lower-than-average testosterone production may find themselves drawn to women who are less feminine and more dominating and dominant in the relationship.

Since a lot of guys produce normal or high amounts of testosterone, even if American men's average testosterone levels have dramatically decreased over the past 50 years, if you're seeking to attract a macho guy, he'd probably like you if your conduct is more feminine, charming, and girly.

She is attractive and seductive, making her the ideal partner for a genuine guy.

A normal, testosterone-normal male will always find a feminine woman more appealing than a woman who believes femininity is overrated and exhibits characteristics that are often associated with men.

The most obvious evidence of femininity in a girl is her physical attributes, but sometimes it also pays to show more femininity in your actions. No, I'm not suggesting perfumed paper and pink frills. However, there are always various approaches to make yourself seem prettier and entice a man to glance at you again and again.

Why do boys like beautiful girls?

Men have historically been the human species' more violent gender. The majority of the time, especially during arguments or whenever they encounter someone they see as a danger in any way, they are the ones that stretch their legs wider, stand taller, and enlarge their chest in an effort to look intimidating.

But being a woman alters everything. A man's protective instincts are triggered when a woman acts in a sweet and feminine way. A feminine female doesn't make him feel intimidated; on the contrary, he feels vulnerable and protective of her. He feels more manly as a result, and every male enjoys feeling manly.

It's quite difficult for any male to ignore a lady when she shows his feminine side or fails to notice his fragility. And as soon as his mind notices her weakness, it immediately dispels any notions of danger, and his protective side forges a relationship of security and attachment with her.

His subconscious mind works extremely hard to make her feel safe, secure, and loved around her because he feels the urge to be around her.

He no longer adopts an aggressive attitude; his voice softens, and instead of opening wide, his shoulders sag down towards her. And he would understand that he already liked the girl before he ever considered attraction!

Use these 34 effective but adorable methods to flirt with a man and bring out his masculinity if you're unsure how to speak to him in a way that brings out this protectiveness.

Characteristics of a charming, feminine lady that appeal to men

Many ladies reject the notion of being too feminine or acting in a nice way when it comes to learning how to attract a guy. A typical contemporary lady sees coyness and modest behavior as signs of weakness. And they find it incomprehensible that a guy finds a pretty female more appealing than a girl who prefers to play the role of a man in a relationship.

You don't actually need to be adorable or behave foolishly if you're feminine. You may just be who you are! However, if you can show a man more of your feminine qualities, it will only enhance your appeal and increase your attractiveness to guys.

Try to watch how a girl behaves rather than looking down on her because she thinks she's pretty or acts adorable. The majority of feminine women are not timid or foolish, and they do not need to act like ignorant bimbos in order to gain a man's admiration.

They only flaunt their femininity and elegance, which are what distinguish women from men. With that simple behavioral change, they eventually transform into ladies who can dominate strong men and wrap them around their tiny pinky.

And no testosterone-laden man can resist the pull of a feminine female when he's conversing with her.From their charming faces, the way they nod their heads, how they behave while speaking with a guy, and the way they grin coyly yet so warmly, everything about them makes them seem more attractive and feminine.

Most females are innately feminine, yet it is a skill that can be developed. You just need to show off your feminine side while speaking to guys if you want to learn how to attract them. And after you give it a try, you'll understand what I mean.

And keep in mind that while attempting to attract the attention of a manly guy, a lovely female who shows off her feminine side will always have an advantage over all other girls! Do you want to know how to be more feminine without trying? You'll be able to draw guys to you without even trying if you follow these 25 methods for looking adorable and feminine!

For the majority of women, femininity is innate. But your actions might make you seem charming.

How to organically bring out your feminine side

There are numerous things you can do easily if you want to come across as a female who is in touch with her femininity when spending time with a guy!

1. If you're wanting to attract a man, talk in a gentle voice.

2. Create more smiles. A grin may improve your demeanor and friendliness.

3. Gently run your fingers through your hair. always effective for males!

4. When you smile or blush, tilt your head slightly lower and give him the look from behind your eyebrow.

These four straightforward suggestions can seem strange to someone who dislikes showing off "girly" characteristics, but they will work wonders for your date!

You may be wondering why we haven't provided more advice on seducing guys here. That's because LovePanky already has a large number of them. We want you to comprehend exactly what is most effective when learning how to attract a guy with the least amount of effort possible.

Don't believe you're a flirtatious girl, but wouldn't you want to learn how to flirt? Talk like you usually would, but with a few flirtatious changes. Use this advice on how to flirt with a man without really flirting!

How to get guys to like you:

Be better while being true to yourself. Contrary to what many think, don't be you. Evolve.

Being yourself isn't always the best strategy for attracting people, despite what some people may tell you. We all undergo constant change. And not all of the changes we see in ourselves may be for the better.

So who are you? What would you say about yourself? Our financial situation, the individuals in our immediate environment, social media, your present aspirations and needs, and other influences from throughout our lives all contribute to who we are. We all undergo constant change; in fact, you are not the same person you were a year ago.

While a select few may have had the good fortune to learn from ideal role models, the majority of us must alter in order to improve as people. Or, even worse, since we believe we are all already flawless, we never get the chance to improve as people or realize our full potential. Because we have strong convictions and refuse to change no matter what, we are stubborn.

Instead of changing who you are solely to appeal to guys, work on improving yourself. Have you ever entered a room full of lovely ladies and felt as though some of them were superior to you in some way?

It only means you admire and desire some particular quality about a woman that you yourself lack when you first meet her, for any reason.

If you admire a quality in a friend, such as her courage, spontaneity, carefree attitude, posture, or fashion sense, your mind may subtly admire that quality because you aspire to possess it. When you notice something you like and want to see it in yourself, a change of this kind is beneficial.

A girl who is the pinnacle of beauty in every manner (if she does exist) won't be awestruck by anybody else. On the other hand, she would always be the girl who would draw admiring glances, curious looks, and gaping mouths everywhere she went!

So change regularly, become the ideal lady you daydream about in your thoughts, and be the person you truly want to be. And everything in your life including guys, career, friends, and everything else will wind up being a lot better for you.

It's simple to dismiss a concept by assuming it's terrible to be feminine or that changing is a negative thing. But change is beneficial. Change is also inescapable. Whether you like it or not, you will change. And you have the option of improving yourself or degrading yourself.

The last word on the science behind sex attraction

Don't forget that we are all animals. Even though we may be walking on two feet or wearing pants (or skirts!), our instincts are still primal. Like animals in the wild, we still pursue and court one another.

Still today, both sexes compete in games to gain each other's favor. Human males still like winning a woman over with displays of their physical prowess, dominance, or sheer magnificence. A guy with excess levels of masculine hormones also prefers elegant, feminine women because they make him feel more manly on the inside.

You don't have to act like the "weaker" sex or seem stupid or weak in order to attract a guy. How in the world did femininity ever come to be seen as "weaker" in the first place?

You only need to embrace your femininity and show off your feminine side while allowing the guy you admire to luxuriate in his manliness and flaunt his masculinity.

Chapter 2

What guys find sexy: quick techniques to get his attention

You may use these pointers and techniques to attract the person you've been admiring from across the room.

Men may be hard to read; let's face it. Although it's best to avoid trickery, there are several techniques to get a guy's attention if you have your eye on him.

Here are some relationship and matchmaking specialists' best advice and techniques for getting a guy to pay close attention to you.

1. Smile

Go to cheerful areas where you know there are males. A lady who is enjoying herself and unwinding will get a man's attention.

2. Avoid hiding in a corner.

Avoid hiding behind pieces of furniture or plants in a corner. If you find something beneficial to do wherever you are (whether it's contributing to a group discussion or slyly making your way to the bar), guys will notice you're being active and not attempting to play hide and seek.

3. Request his aid.

Despite how retro this may seem, guys really like being helpful. Tell him about a difficult issue at work or ask for his advice on a new app. Tessina. That being said, the best way to influence him is to be helpful.

Consider what you might ask him that will make him feel smarter than his stomach.

4. Discuss your interests.

Discuss the little things you do, such as having fresh flowers in your house, doing yoga, reading a book every week, or getting a good night's sleep. Despite their seeming insignificance, it is reassuring to find any indication of a grounded and balanced way of living.

5. Avoid dressing for your girlfriends.

You should keep your off-the-shoulder, ruffled crop top for a girl's night out since guys don't comprehend fashion trends. The easiest method to get a man's attention is to dress elegantly in a timeless ensemble that you are certain will flatter you.

6. Observe him intently.

Tessina and Hahn both advise making some traditional, direct eye contact. (However, avoid staring them down.) Don't be afraid to flirt across the room with his eyes to let him know you're interested.

7. Don't state the obvious.

Don't name drop. You shouldn't mention the brand if a guy praises anything you're wearing since it could make you seem conceited. You should say you're glad they noticed and go on to another subject.

The same is true for dining and drinking establishments; even if you visit the hippest pubs and eateries, you should speak about less well-known places. Being eccentric will make for a more fascinating conversation than coming off as an expert.

8. Go out by yourself or with a single buddy.

When going out, Tessina warns against hanging out with a gaggle of chicks. If you're among a group, it will be difficult to isolate you.

If you do go out with a group, make an effort to stand out or figure out how to spend some time by yourself.

By contributing to the discussion the man you have your eye on is having, you may demonstrate that you have something attractive about yourself and that you are more than simply a pretty face. We now place such a strong emphasis on appearances that Tessina said that it was pleasant to witness a lady who was as entertaining as she was fascinating.

9. **Express gratitude**

The owners of the dating service Project Soulmate, Lori Zaslow and Jenn Zucher, claim that men are truly irritated when women don't express gratitude. Even the most self-assured man values a sincere thank you.You don't even need to say it out loud; just send him your number when he gives you a drink. It just seems nicer to put it in writing, and it's such a simple way to show someone how much you appreciate them.

10. **Put down the phone.**

It's a tiny world, so you never know who you could run into when you're busy Instagramming your oysters. Try not to stare at your phone when on the elevator and instead glance around to see who is around. For a male, seeing a lady who isn't engrossed in Snapchat or snapping a selfie is pleasant.

11. **Express your passions at the bar.**

Bring a book to read while you drink. "Give him a special reason to approach you," said Emma Tessler, creator of the dating business The Dating Ring. Bring a sketchbook, notebook, or whatever pastime you like doing when you don't feel like reading.

12. **Don trendy jewelry**

Men will want to comment or ask you questions, so if you're wearing something flashy and noticeable, he can use that as a conversation starter. Put on your largest ring or your most unique earrings to accomplish two goals at once: to have a nice accent for your clothing and to engage someone in discussion.

Chapter 3

10 Secrets from the Science of Attraction on How to Attract Men

Do you ever feel as if you lack the necessary dating skills?

As if you're aware that something is wrong but aren't sure what it is?

Have you ever seen two strangers interact and been immediately intrigued? Or have you ever observed a pair out on a date and questioned how they ended up together?

The answer is likely yes if you're like the majority of individuals. But what is it about a person that attracts another? And maybe more significantly, can you master the art of seducing men using the laws of attraction?

1. **Stop wondering now. It's not just you.**

Science describes attraction as a perplexing and complicated phenomenon. However, it doesn't follow that we can't work out certain fundamentals.

This blog article will provide some advice on how to attract guys as well as the science of attraction. Read on. Your romantic situation could improve.

2. Making eye contact

The eyes are the key. Eye contact is critical in first impressions.

Women must have the ability to send the appropriate messages with their eyes in order to attract men. Men may sense your interest in them and be drawn to you if you maintain strong eye contact and initiate eye contact. It's vital to keep in mind that your eyes may convey a lot without speaking, so be careful how you use this potent instrument!

According to studies, males who make more eye contact with other men are seen as being more powerful and dominating. So, try meeting a man's eyes from across the room if you want to interest him.

3. Your appearance

Is there anything worse than showing up to an occasion underdressed?

You feel uncomfortable, your date feels uncomfortable, and you can even get the stigma of being a snob as a result.

So how can you avoid these pitfalls and dress in a way that appeals to men? Exposing some flesh is a huge help.

But be careful not to overdo it! Men like women who wear skirts, dresses, high heels, etc., but they like them much more when they wear these items sparingly.

When you constantly expose too much flesh, you resemble a wealthy call girl. Wear something that is flattering for your body type and appealing to guys in general, but avoid dressing primarily to attract males.

If you're looking for a guy, it may be worthwhile to experiment with different outfit styles.Here are some pointers on how to entice guys with your sense of style. Put on clothing that suits you nicely and highlights your best features. Use apparel with words on it sparingly. These tend to annoy men a bit since they might seem sexist.

4. **Your Cologne**

Don't we all want to know how to seduce men?

And when it comes to attractiveness, what comes to mind for the majority of people? Of course, I mean how you look! But did you realize that something as basic as your perfume may greatly influence a man's attraction to you?

Surprisingly, the scent you wear could make or break your chances of having other sex.So if you're trying to increase your attractiveness, start by focusing on your odor. Here are some suggestions on how to change your fragrance and become unstoppable!

Do you recall high school? Or every time you were surrounded by adolescent boys acting out due to their hormones? Boys' noses are, as we all know, essentially attached to the backs of girls' blouses.

5. **Smile**

Men are naturally attracted to joyful women. One of a woman's most effective weapons for drawing attention from men is her smile.

Men perceive warmth, pleasure, and confidence to be alluring attributes that are all communicated by a smile. In fact, Manchester University research indicated that people are seen as more beautiful when they smile than when they don't.

Women who grin are more likely to attract males than those who don't. The act of smiling made them seem less frightening and more accessible since it was seen as non-threatening.

So show off your sparkling teeth to start attracting guys!

6. **Your hair**

Unbelievably, your hair may also make you more attractive to guys! Your hairstyle gives the world information about who you are and what you desire. It may read, "I'm a high-class girl who can take care of herself," or "I'm a wild youngster who is eager for some fun."

So think about switching up your hair the next time you want to attract guys! Here are some suggestions for haircuts that appeal to men:

Try putting your hair down if you want to draw in males. A slight curl may be seen in hair that has been worn down; this conveys warmth and approachability. The smooth neck skin of women also gives them a more attractive appearance than men.

7. The quantity of makeup you use

Trying to entice men? Perhaps you might start by applying cosmetics. Men find women who wear more makeup to be more appealing.
So, if you want to get a date, don't be scared to wear some blush and eyeliner. Just be careful not to overdo it since wearing too much makeup might have the opposite effect and make you seem less appealing. Too much makeup could come across as artificial and mask-like.
Try several things until you discover what suits you best, and keep in mind that confidence is essential.

8. Developing intimacy too quickly

Men are naturally drawn to close physical contact. In reality, a lot of men tend to be attracted to women who are eager to engage in immediate physical intimacy.

Though initially pleasing, this might potentially lead to issues in the future. Here are some reasons why having too much intimacy too soon might be problematic and some tips on how to attract guys without putting yourself in danger.

What's wrong with getting too personal too soon?

A guy believes he doesn't have to commit if you get intimate with him too fast. Why would he, too? You are already willing to spend the night with him, after all.

A subtle way to say "I'm not picky" is to get personal too quickly. This tells men that you won't be a demanding spouse, so they don't have to make a commitment.

How do I entice guys without having an immediate sexual encounter?

Having said that, it's crucial to not fully hold off on your guy. If you reject any kind of physical intimacy before being married, it might be an indication that there are issues in the relationship.

The secret is to strike a balance. However, don't hold back on basic physical intimacy like holding hands or going into bed too quickly.

9. Your own style

When it comes to establishing a strong first impression, confidence is essential.

How you present yourself greatly influences how appealing you are to guys. Men will be attracted to you if you seem confident and at ease in your own skin. You can do a few things to improve your attractiveness.

Here are some pointers on how to use your body language to entice men: Do not cross your arms. Don't be afraid to look a man in the eye while you're speaking to him. Stand tall with your shoulders back and your feet about shoulder width apart. When speaking to men, convey an attitude of openness.

10. What You Say

So, you're hoping to draw in some guys, right?

The first thing to note is that a key component is how you speak. Here are three suggestions to help you make your words work for you if you want to capture and hold his attention.

Be honest first. You don't have to pretend to be someone you're not to get his attention. He will really recognize it right away. Keep your outlook up, second. Although you may believe that being difficult to get would make him like you more, this strategy often backfires. Finally, stop using pickup lines and clichés. They may be effective at times (which is fine), but they can also come across as forced and phony.Keep it natural and use your own words.

11. **Your Attitude**

You need to have the appropriate attitude if you want to attract guys. It's crucial to project confidence and optimism around guys, since they are attracted to women who do these things.

It's no secret that guys are drawn to women who exude confidence. It's crucial to have the appropriate attitude if you want to attract a guy. You should behave as if you know what you want and that you're worth pursuing, without seeming haughty or conceited.

Here are some pointers for using your attitude to attract men:

1. Trust in your abilities. Women who have confidence in themselves and their talents appeal to men. He will question himself if you do.

2. Be upbeat. Men find optimistic attitudes appealing because they think you're carefree and cheerful.

3. Avoid becoming desperate or needy. Try to avoid coming off as too eager or reliant on him, since neediness is a big turnoff for most guys.

4. Show Feminism. It's attractive to see a lady with a strong personality, but don't lose your femininity. Men like a woman

who exudes confidence and kindness while being able to lower her guard and show vulnerability in his presence.

Chapter 4

Men's Priorities in a Relationship

What each sex believes the other sex wants from them and what the other sex really wants are in striking contrast, I've found.

Women often harbor bitterness and animosity toward men as a result of what they believe men want from them, which makes them doubt their ability to ever have a good, loving, passionate relationship. Men often experience similar emotions and anger about what they believe women want from them. If only we would acknowledge that both men and women are human beings with essentially similar desires. You don't, however, have to believe me since I've spoken with a lot of men and women who are actively interested in their own personal development to find out what they need in a relationship. You'll be surprised by their responses.

Find out what guys claim to desire from women and compare it to what women believe men want. You'll also receive advice on how women may satisfy men's desires, locate a nice guy to date, and build a lovely relationship.

1. **For men, honest communication is of the utmost importance.**

They are looking for a lady who is honest in her responses and can even provide information.They want a woman who assertively requests that her desires and needs be satisfied. They are looking for a lady who can communicate with compassion while seeing reality and telling it like it is. Men desire a partner who can converse without being overly critical and who values maintaining their dignity. Women believe that men want them to be superficial, keep their needs and wants to themselves, and never make demands. Women believe that men just want them to grow up because they find them to be too needy and sensitive. Some women think they don't have the right to speak up because they fear being rejected if they do.

A piece of advice for women

Great men desire and require open, fearless communication without anger or judgment. One way to attract a fantastic guy and establish a successful relationship is to learn how to express your truth and wants effectively.

2. Men want self-sufficient, secure, and confident women.

Men like it when a woman chooses them out of "desire" rather than out of emotional or pecuniary desperation. Men desire and need their relationships, but they also want their lovers to be someone apart from them. Men want dynamic, independent women who have their own hobbies and friends. However, men value the time they spend with a caring companion. Women believe that men don't want them to depend on them. Women believe that men don't value or require quality time with their partners. Women think that making a guy feel wanted would make him uncomfortable and could even cause him to flee.

A piece of advice for women

Men want a whole companion, just as women do. Making a rich, fulfilling life for your own happiness is one effective technique to attract a fantastic guy and develop a strong connection.

3. Men want a relationship free of manipulation.

No form of manipulation is what men seek. They don't want to have to attempt to decipher signals or read their partner's thoughts. They do not want to be pressured into a relationship before they are ready. They do not want to be forced into accepting full responsibility for everything that goes wrong. They do not want to be the target of gamesmanship. Women believe that men prefer little to no communication and that the only way to satisfy desires is through manipulation.Women believe that men either need or want reminders that the relationship must progress. Women often solely express verbal criticism because they believe that men don't respect or desire praise and appreciation.

A piece of advice for women

Men will not tolerate manipulation of any kind for any significant length of time. (1) Develop the ability to ask for what you want and need in every aspect of your life without hesitation in order to attract a fantastic guy and create a good relationship. (2) Become more conscious of his timing and timetable. (3) develop the ability to provide and accept compliments.

4. **Men wish to grow, take personal responsibility, and own.**

Men want a mate who is courageous and strong yet also knows how to laugh at herself. They want a woman who understands and accepts her role in the dynamics of relationships. She must possess emotional stability. Men want a woman who is growing personally and who takes ownership of her emotional experiences. Women believe that men are solely interested in having fun. Women believe that men are not interested in establishing and maintaining healthy relationships or in improving their own lives. Women believe that men only want supermodel-like women and that they never take a woman's emotional maturity, kindness, support, or love into account.

A piece of advice for women

Men want women who are emotionally mature. Lack of emotion does not equate to maturity. It does refer to the capacity for responsible emotional management. Learn to be in control of your emotional experience and expression if you want to find a fantastic guy and establish a lasting relationship.

5. Men want commitment to the relationship and fidelity.

Integrity is a must-have. In reality, males prefer partners who can fully commit to the relationship and don't have "roaming eyes." Many people describe commitment as being faithful and ready to work on the relationship, even when things are difficult. Women believe that men just want sex and would leave a relationship for a woman with a more attractive face. Women think men cannot be trusted to be faithful. Women believe men do not want to work on a relationship and that when the going gets tough, they run.

A piece of advice for women

Here is some great news for those women who are resigned to the myth that all men cheat: infidelity and "a roaming eye" are as distasteful to men as they are to women. Great men know how to build a wonderful relationship, and they know fidelity is the main ingredient.

6. Men want women who know how men need to be treated.

Many women treat men in ways that diminish their egos, making them feel inadequate. Men would rather have more praise, more acknowledgment of what they do right, and recognition that they are great guys who are loved and appreciated. Women believe that men do not regard a woman's advice, encouragement, or admiration. Women criticize because they feel that many of the things that are important to them are not important to men. Criticism may be a means to voice displeasure.

A piece of advice for women

Most guys seek attention and praise from women. Learning to recognize your spouse instead of making them wrong is one of the most significant relationship survival techniques accessible to you.

Chapter 5

8 characteristics of women that draw and hold a man

Wouldn't it be fantastic to have the ability to attract pretty much any male she wanted? Men may be picky when it comes to dating, as anybody who is single is likely aware. Like women, males often have an idealized image of the ideal woman to whom they are drawn.

Most of the time, you either meet or exceed their expectations. However, males sometimes fall for women who are outside of their comfort zone, just as women do. You want to be in a committed relationship, but you often question how to entice a guy into a committed relationship or marriage.

Be less concerned. You may use a few simple strategies to draw in the kind of guy you want to date. This article discusses eight of these traits that men value in a woman. On the basis of it, you may attempt to address your "how to attract guys" question.

Read on!

1. Living a life apart from a romantic connection

Men are particularly drawn to independent women who lead independent lifestyles. Therefore, the next time you notice the man you truly like calling, resist the urge to pick up and return his call.

Being confident in your own skin, independent, and not always clinging to your partner are the keys to understanding how to draw in and maintain a man.

Guys detest being ignored, but they also dislike clinging girls. So have a life, get out with your girlfriends, and sometimes brush him off. Many guys like the thrill of the hunt, and they'll pursue you even harder.

They are drawn to you even more since you are a busy woman with a full schedule of activities.

2. Suspicious

Do you ever find yourself telling him everything about your life on a first date? If so, you may wish to exercise self-control. He could flee as a result of his actions. Men like ladies who maintain a little facade.
They struggle mightily to get part of that barricade to crumble since they never know what's on their minds.
Men are curious about whatever secrets you could have, and they won't let up until they do. Give him information sparingly rather than everything at once.

3. Positivity

Men like women who are at ease with themselves. How do you then draw in the appropriate guys while avoiding the incorrect ones?
Be yourself and exude confidence. Narcissistic males often search for women who can boost their egos and

give them ongoing self-confidence. Such women may struggle with confidence or believe it is unattractive for them to be openly proud of who they are.

You'll find a decent man if you project confidence. a healthy person without any warped ulterior motives.

Women who are self-assured are aware of their life goals and are unwilling to postpone achieving them by hanging out with men.They are eager to improve their deficiencies since they are aware of them. They also take great pride in their abilities.

Women may now feel secure in their lives and in their relationships as a result. Men find it appealing that they don't want to spend time playing games.

4. Self care

If you do not believe in taking care of yourself, how can you attract men? "You can't," is the response.

Perhaps the one thing that counts the most to men is this. It's not about applying a pound of cosmetics to our faces while spending hours in front of the mirror.

Neither is it about being the room's thinnest girl.

So, how can a woman entice a man without obsessing about her looks or adhering to false notions of beauty propagated by the media?

It's about maintaining the wellness of our bodies and minds as well as our skin and hair. Whether or not we have a partner in our life, it is imperative that we love ourselves enough to take care of ourselves. Men don't criticize women as quickly as they do, but we (women) can be our own harshest critics at times.

5. avoids dwelling on the past

Everybody has a history, and that past contributes to who we are now. The past is left in the past for a reason, however. A guy can only take so much of a woman's ranting about her controlling parents, emotionally abusive ex-lover, or former partners.

Being respectful and thoughtful enough to accept your history without bringing it up in every discussion with the guy you are presently dating is the easy solution to the issue of how to attract men.

The manner in which you discuss your previous relationships with him will have a significant impact on how to draw a wonderful man. The relationship will undoubtedly end badly if you keep raving about your ex or bringing up old dates and tales from your previous relationship.

A woman who recognizes her history but doesn't linger on her faults, failures, or unpleasant experiences with her ex is attractive to a guy.

Women who live in the past have a tendency to compare their present relationships to their previous ones and search for parallels. Instead of concentrating on the past, pay attention to the present. Just as much as women hate being compared to their ex-partners, so do men.

6. Attention to detail

Being watchful is a sure way to attract and keep guys interested in you!

Even though it's crucial to have hobbies that are all your own, paying attention to your man's interests may make him feel loved and appreciated.

If you despise basketball, this does not obligate you to support his preferred basketball team. Additionally, it does not obligate you to share all of his hobbies.

But being able to talk with him sometimes about his interests will show him that you are interested in him enough to do some research.

How do you keep a guy in love with you and prevent a deterioration in your relationship?

It's an easy remedy. Start by getting to know him better and gauging his interests. Your boyfriend will start returning the favor after you do this and feel that connection. For example, he could start noticing your new hairstyle or asking about your ladies' night out.

7. Irregularity

You girls need to stop thinking like Prince Charming in your attempts to attract men!

There is no such thing, if you hadn't already guessed that. That's like your partner comparing you to a princess who uses rollers in her hair and goes to bed every night wearing a green face mask. Yet so many women make an effort to shape their partner into the "ideal man" they have in mind. These ladies must keep in mind that individuals only alter their behavior when they choose to.

They must comprehend that it is our diversity that defines who we are. You adore your partner for all of his good and bad qualities when you fall in love with him. Why wouldn't you embrace your differences today if you already did so in the beginning? A woman who seeks to alter a man's identity is intolerable to men. Be grateful for all of his efforts, great or small, therefore.

8. Sincerity

How can I find a nice guy to marry or to commit to in a committed, long-term relationship? A good partnership cannot exist without honest, open communication.

Men dislike playing games or reading minds. Being truthful with her man is thus the best thing a woman can do.Men dislike it when women use contradictory language. They would rather we express our anger openly than have them guess what we are upset about.

Additionally, it allows us to make clear what we do and do not desire. Due to our poor ability to infer one another's perspectives, men and women often miscommunicate with one another. Nothing damages or destroys a relationship more quickly than a persistent misunderstanding.

You may now find out how to attract the right guy for marriage by giving up on attempting to make your partner strain to play psychic and simply being honest with him.

Chapter 6

10 Attractive Physical Qualities for Women: What men find most physically appealing

When it comes to dating, particularly with men, appearances always count. Men have always been and will always be visual beings. However, most men have a tendency to be rather amenable and also have a favorite body part or physical trait that makes them weak in the knees.

Have you ever pondered what physically appeals to men and what draws all the males to the yard? So, you can stop wondering. You may learn all there is to know about what attracts guys in this essay.

1. Booty

Look, guys have long been known to fixate on women's behinds. Men's desire for women with huge behinds is physiologically predisposed, partly because it is an indication of health. Guys are more likely to notice you if your butt is bigger. Even if they won't say it, the majority of guys like booty.

2. Breasts

No, having enormous breasts won't make a man pay attention to you. In actuality, most men choose breasts that are average to somewhat smaller in size. Your options are open as long as they are attractive and vivacious.

3. Legs

A nice set of legs, especially toned ones, can turn the heads of many guys. Like with booty, most men unconsciously interpret powerful legs as a sign of health, which piques their attention.

4. Eyes

The eyes do indeed have it. Many men will notice a woman's eye before her physique, which may surprise you. By the way, using mascara has been proven to greatly increase how appealing men find you sexually and is also known to make you seem younger. Therefore, having eyes is undoubtedly a benefit.

5. Lips

You know, lip gloss and lipstick were created for a purpose. Men certainly like examining a woman's lips, particularly if they are full and youthful-looking.

6. Smooth skin

Ladies, acne is never attractive. Men enjoy clear skin and they love it even more if it's silky. Just about everyone finds someone with regular facials, occasional trips to the dermatologist, and generally healthy-looking skin to be quite attractive.

7. **For some men, well-styled hair is their kryptonite.**

This is especially true if the men in question have a soft spot for a certain shade of hair. Speaking from experience as someone who often colors their hair an odd shade of red or punk, having a certain attractive haircut would undoubtedly get attention from men.

8. **Clean hands, feet, and nails**

You're mistaken if you believe that men don't care about manicures and pedicures. The most widespread kink in the world is foot fetishism, which is also the only non-sexual body component to actually appear in porn searches. Thus, those excursions to the salon will undoubtedly catch the attention of guys.

9. **Your height**

Men have long been known to be drawn to women with hourglass figures, particularly if they are on the leaner side of things. Fortunately, if it's truly that essential to you, there are techniques to hide your body's appearance or even shed weight.

10. **A grin.**

A beautiful grin can make any female seem like a model and, to a certain extent, may also make a girl appear more accessible and flirtatious. A frown often means "Leave me alone," meanwhile. So, if you want to know what men find physically attractive, a grin may be a powerful man-magnet.

How to Make Your Man Content in a Relationship, Both Emotionally and Sexually

Making your boyfriend emotionally and sexually satisfied is not always simple to do in a relationship. You must pay attention to his wants and know when to give him space if you want to make your partner emotionally content. You must be eager to take risks and be brave and adventurous in order to satisfy your boyfriend sexually. However, what matters most is that you are enjoying yourself as you win over your boyfriend. Simply follow these instructions to learn how to make your boyfriend feel emotionally and sexually satisfied in a relationship.

Method 1.

Make your man emotionally happy

Recognize your man's mood swings. Men have the same potential for moodiness as women. You must become familiar with your man's emotions in order to know what to do to make him feel emotionally happy. Spending more time with your boyfriend can help you better understand his emotions and let you respond more swiftly when they arise. As you come to know your man's moods, keep the following in mind:

If you try to console him when he's unhappy and wants to talk to you rather than when he's brooding and wants to be left alone, you'll either suffocate him or alienate him.

Just be patient with him if he's feeling irritable due to traffic or a poor performance in a basketball game. It's not the right moment to begin kissing him or to start chatting up your pals.

Wait till your partner is in a good mood if you want to have a "serious chat" with him. You will not get the desired results if you bring up a serious issue while he is stressed and has a lot on his plate.

1. **Motivate him.**

You must know how to inspire your boyfriend in a sincere manner if you want to make him emotionally happy.

You may support him in following his ambitions and aspirations by complimenting him on how great, talented, or funny he is. When you support him in moving ahead in life, you must be honest; don't just say you're encouraging him.

Bake him cookies or give him a call the night before his big basketball game to let him know you care.

Praise him and let him know how great he is before a major exam, interview, or other crucial occasion so he feels confident.

2. **Express your admiration for him without going crazy.**

You should express your feelings to a guy, whether you love him or simply really like him, in order to make him emotionally happy. When you bid your boyfriend farewell, tell him that you adore him or think he's fantastic, and every time you hang out, find at least one reason to commend him. You can express your admiration for him without being overbearing or overwhelming him.

You don't need to contact him 20 times a day to tell him how gorgeous he is or how excited you are to meet him; this will only overwhelm him.

Make sure the love is reciprocal. You may have a problem if you compliment him often yet get no reaction.

3. **Try not to clutch too much.**

You must be able to support your guy when he needs you and step back and give him space when he needs it if you want to make him emotionally happy. Clinginess is wanting to be with him all the time, not allowing him to spend time with his sons, and checking in every fifteen seconds when he isn't there. Who likes that now? No one.

No matter how committed you are to one another, you shouldn't have to sleep together every night. Have fun going out with your ladies, and don't interfere when he goes out with his lads.

You can phone him once or twice if you're not hanging out together that day, but avoid calling him often, particularly if you know he's with his buddies, since this will bother him.

You must be able to follow your own hobbies, have your own passions, and be yourself without the man's assistance if you really want to quit being attached. The time you spend with your partner should be enjoyable, but he shouldn't be the center of your existence.

4. **Become a good compromiser.**

You must be able to make concessions when you disagree if you want to make your boyfriend emotionally content. You should be aware that you should both be able to achieve your objectives or reach an agreement that allows you to both get something that makes you happy.Understanding how to compromise means being able to consider both your own and your partner's interests anytime you make a choice.

You might also alternate who gets what; for example, on a date night, you can choose the restaurant and he might choose the movie.

Don't be one of those women who always gets what she wants because her spouse finds it simpler to grant her wishes than to fight for them.

Both parties in a healthy relationship should be open to making concessions.

Instead of screaming at each other when you disagree, practice having calm conversations.

5. Selecting conflicts should be avoided.

Nothing annoys a guy more than getting into a fight, argument, or disagreement with his lady for no reason.If you need to talk to him about anything important, choose a time and location where you can both concentrate on the topic. Do not start screaming at him in front of other people and then expect him to respond. When you disagree, practice not raising your voice but rather keeping it cool.

If you feel the need to start a quarrel, consider why you want to start the fight and what is actually making you furious. You need to find a mature approach to talking about this.

6. Don't ask him if he's angry with you if he's just having a bad day.

This is a typical error that many women commit. If your guy is clearly irritable and you don't know why he is, or even if you do, you know you can't cure it, so you may be tempted to inquire, "Are you upset with me?" "Is it a comment I made?" This will simply make the man feel worse if he already has a terrible attitude and has no legitimate reason to be angry with you.

You must be aware that there are certain circumstances you just cannot control. His life doesn't revolve around you, so if he's having a terrible day, he's simply having a bad day.

7. Keep having fun in mind.

Some women are so consumed by the idea of having the ideal relationship that they neglect to unwind and just enjoy their spouse. Although establishing a solid, loving relationship is important, partnerships also need the ability to laugh, be silly, and enjoy themselves without exerting too much effort. If you two don't often laugh together, your boyfriend can't be emotionally content.

Don't stress too much about organizing the ideal date or romantic activity. The most enjoyable activities include watching a silly movie, hanging out at the mall, and going to the beach on a whim.

Method 2.

Make your man sexually happy

1. Be able to touch him.

You must understand how to touch a guy sensually in order to arouse him if you want to be able to make him happy sexually. Although every guy is unique, practically every man has a number of places where he would like to be stroked to set the mood. Here are a few places to look for love:
Using your lips, lightly touch his inner ear, touch him behind his ear, or murmur into it.
Kiss his neck, nipping just a little bit on the front and back. Try giving him a seductive shoulder rub to see if it sparks anything more. When you kiss him, softly stroke the back of his head. While you're speaking, place your hand on the small of his back. Place a hard palm on his chest.

2. **Examine various sex positions.**

You cannot consistently perform the same thing if you want to satisfy your man's sexual needs. You should be open to doing new things and experimenting in different roles as long as you feel comfortable doing so. If you usually kiss with him on top of you, consider switching it up so that you're on the bottom. The same is true for having intercourse.

Be open to the process, even if not every new experience you have will be enjoyable. You may return to your former favorite spots while experimenting with new ideas.

Allow him to set the pace. Perhaps he knows what he wants. If not, you should first try something else.

3. **Establish new connections.**

You shouldn't always hook up in the same spot on your bed if you want to keep your boyfriend satisfied. Instead, consider walking around your house or apartment and exploring every nook and cranny with your body.If you choose to hook up outside the house, whether you stay in a hotel in your hometown or go on a romantic getaway, don't be scared to do it.

Never undervalue a makeout at a movie theater. Another enduring favorite is kissing while driving. Sex up in public. Find a nice, isolated area, and enjoy yourself with your guy.

4. Take risks.

You need to be daring if you want to satisfy your boyfriend sexually. This entails having the courage to explore new locales and engage in novel experiences whenever the mood strikes. Being adventurous means being open to trying new activities, such as skinny dipping, beach kissing, or spending a long night in bed with someone when out on a weekend walk.

Instead of coming up with excuses not to try anything new, consider all the pleasure that may be had.

Take a last-minute weekend getaway. Drive to your selected location by pointing your finger at it on the map. Enjoy getting to know each other's bodies as well as the new location.

5. **Be brave.**

Another technique for satisfying your boyfriend sexually is to be brave. To be brave, you must tell your guy what and when you want. Take command of the evening, bring your boyfriend into the bedroom, and give him detailed instructions. You may even turn to him in the midst of a party or busy bar and hushedly say, "I want you," assuring him that it's time to get home and be together right now.

Your courage and honesty will be appreciated by your boyfriend, and it will make him more attracted to you.

Go for it if you're feeling it. If your partner is taking a shower and you start to feel particularly lovable, simply slip in and join him for a soap session.

6. **Be obscene.**

If you sometimes act raunchy, your boyfriend will adore you for it. You must be willing to push the boundaries of your sexuality if you want to be filthy. Here are some examples of filthy behavior:

No matter how ludicrous it may be, go to a sex shop and get some whips, sex toys, and provocative attire.

Purchase some really seductive, see-through underwear.

Have fun exchanging naughty texts or phone calls with your partner to make him think of you while you're not there. He will adore it.

Method 3

Keep Him Content

1. Keep your bond vibrant.

Even if you've been together for years, you can't simply fall into the same old pattern if you want to keep your boyfriend satisfied sexually and emotionally. Both of you will lose interest if you don't make an effort to keep things interesting.

At least once every month, engage in a novel activity as a couple. It could include motorcycling, beach volleyball, or rock climbing.

Together, attend a dancing lesson. You'll be able to keep your body in tune as you explore new vistas if you learn to salsa or ballroom dance.

Every week, find a fresh way to congratulate your guy. There are constantly more things about him that you adore. Every now and again, play hard to get. He shouldn't think he can have you at any time.

Recognize that the hunt never ends. He ought to be pursuing you with the same zeal he showed on the day you first met.

2. Avoid becoming envious.

Starting to get overwhelmed by envy for no apparent cause is the quickest way to ruin a fantastic relationship. If you act jealous, it will simply irritate and frustrate your boyfriend and give him the impression that you don't trust him enough in the relationship to believe that he won't cheat on you. Even if it's absolutely innocuous, you need to concentrate on controlling your jealousy and giving your partner a sense of security if you can't bear it when he chats with or even brings up another woman.

Your partner will be pleased if you can refrain from talking badly about other females in your social circle.

Knowing that there are many other attractive people of the opposite sex out there and accepting that you won't pursue them is a necessary component of being in a successful relationship. You have a problem if you believe that your partner can't be near an attractive female without making advances.

3. **Don't attempt to alter him.**

Why bother with your boyfriend if you don't like him in some ways?It's OK to want your guy to improve, whether it's by being on time for your dates or returning your calls within three hours, but it's not acceptable to attempt to alter the way your man appears, behaves, thinks, or speaks to fit your ideal of what the "perfect man" should be like. Your guy will just get irritated, feel like he can't be himself, and think that you don't like him for who he really is as a result of this.

It's OK to call attention to your man's undesirable conduct if you see it. But if you criticize him for every little flaw, such as the way he eats his food or laces his shoes, he'll think you're continually bugging him.

Nobody is flawless. You should be aware that your boyfriend may not find everything about you perfect, but that's alright.

4. **Leave him alone.**

Even if you've been together for a long time and share a bed and a house, you should constantly remember to give your boyfriend some space. You should be able to spend some time away from your partner in order for your bond to deepen when you get back together and for you to continue to realize how unique your partners are.

A sign of maturity and trust is being able to let your partner do his own thing on the weekends, go to happy hour with his colleagues without you always being there, or take a weekend trip to see his family.

You won't be able to keep your partner happy for very long if you feel compelled to remain by his side all the time or if you are unable to have fun.

5. **Ensure your happiness.**

Although it's crucial that you meet your man's sexual and emotional needs, it's also crucial that you feel emotionally and sexually satisfied in the relationship. Assuring that the man's wants are addressed is not the woman's responsibility; rather, a solid partnership is built on shared affection, support, and acceptance. You have a problem if you feel that all of your time is spent considering what your guy wants rather than being aware of your own needs.

Even if it's impossible for you and your partner to have complete emotional and sexual satisfaction all the time, you should both be content most of the time if you want your relationship to succeed.